Third picture quiz book

Compiled by Boswell Taylor

Question setter for
BBC Top of the Form
BBC Transworld Top Team
BBC Mastermind

THIRD PICTURE QUIZ BOOK

Compiled by Boswell Taylor

KNIGHT BOOKS

The paperback division of Brockhampton Press

ISBN 0 340 18055 2

First published in 1975 by Knight, the paperback division of
Brockhampton Press Ltd., Salisburv Road, Leicester.

Text copyright © 1975 Boswell Taylor
Illustrations copyright © 1965, 1967, 1968, 1969, 1970,
1971, 1972, 1973, 1974, 1975 Brockhampton Press Ltd.

Printed and bound in Great Britain
by Richard Clay (The Chaucer Press) Ltd., Bungay, Suffolk.

Contents

1 At the fishmonger's

Match the pictures to the names below

Salmon
Red mullet
Pilchard
Halibut
Eel
Crab
Shrimp
Plaice
Herring
Whiting
Lobster
Cod

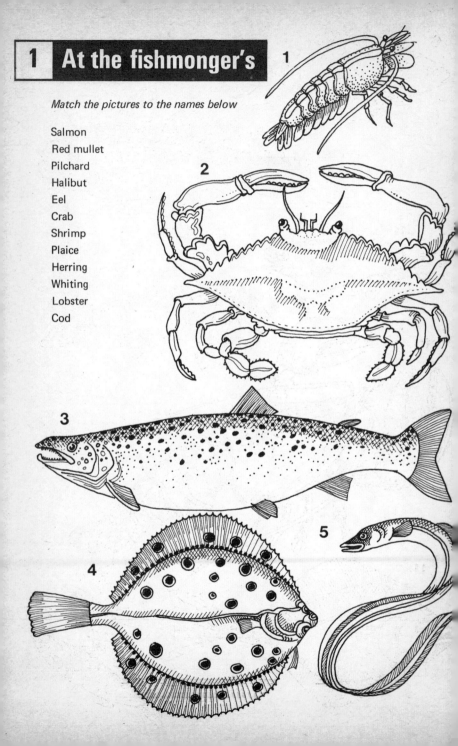

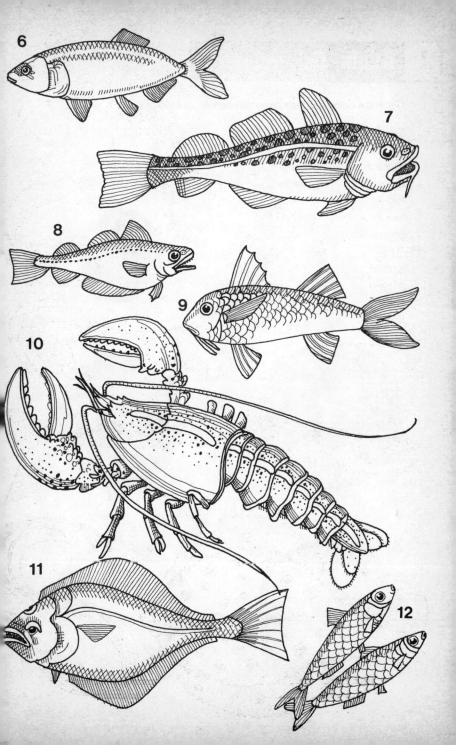

2 Coins

Match these coins to their correct countries listed below

Denmark	The Netherlands
Greece	Luxembourg
Manchuria	Portugal
Switzerland	Lebanon
Turkey	Germany
Italy	Ireland
France	

1

2

3

4

5

3 Homes

Match the pictures to the descriptions
given below

Chinese house
West African stilt house
Norwegian log house
Siberian tent
Mongolian felt yurt tent
Bedouin Arab tent
French château
Wood and plaster house, Cheshire
Queen Anne house
Roman villa

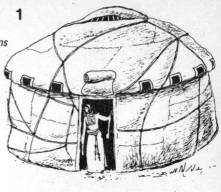

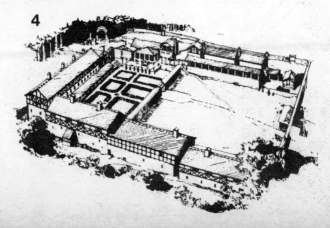

4 Headgear

How would the fashionable lady style her hair?

Miss Roman Empire
Miss Ancient Egypt
Miss Norman
Miss White and Red Rose
Miss Tudor
Miss Elizabeth I
Miss Early Stuart
Miss Late Stuart
Miss Georgian
Miss Early Victorian
Miss Late Victorian

1

2

3

4

5

5 Cavalry

Match the pictures to the names below

Assyrian c. 700 BC
Parthian c. 50 BC
Gothic c. 500 AD
Saxon c. 700 AD
Italian c. 1325
German c. 1480
Japanese c. 1600
British carabineer c. 1600
British dragoon c. 1815
English lancer c. 1850

1

2

3

4

5

6

7

8

9

10

Match the postmarks to the countries below

Poland
Ireland
South Africa
Sweden
Austria
Spain
East Germany
West Germany
Iran

1

2

3

4

5

POLLENSA
23.SET.74
·BALEARES·

6

FRANKFURT AM MAIN
17. 9. 74
6

7

ÅSARNA
22.10.
74
✕

8

23 SRÁID MAC PIARAIS B.Á.C.
24 ✕ ✕
74

9

WASOSZ K GÓRY SI
21 12 73-9
9

7 Countries and counties

Which European countries do these shaded areas represent?

Which counties do these shaded areas represent?

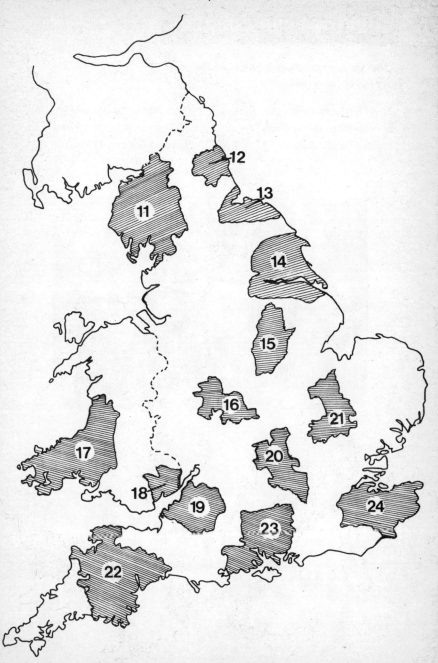

8   Old London

These were landmarks in old London. Match the pictures to the names below

Royal Exchange before the Great Fire   Great Piazza, Covent Garden
St Bride's Church, by Wren   St George's, Hanover Square
Theatre Royal, Drury Lane   Vauxhall Gardens 1765

1

2

Match the pictures to the names below

Jowett 7 hp 1923
Toyota
Rolls Royce 30 hp 1905
Peugeot's 'baby car' 1911
Vauxhall Viva 1966
Ford Popular 1935
First £100 car 1931
Delage-type D8 SS100 1933
Mercedes 300 SL 1955
Lagonda LG 6 1938
OE-type 30/98 Vauxhall 1925
8 hp Lanchester 1897

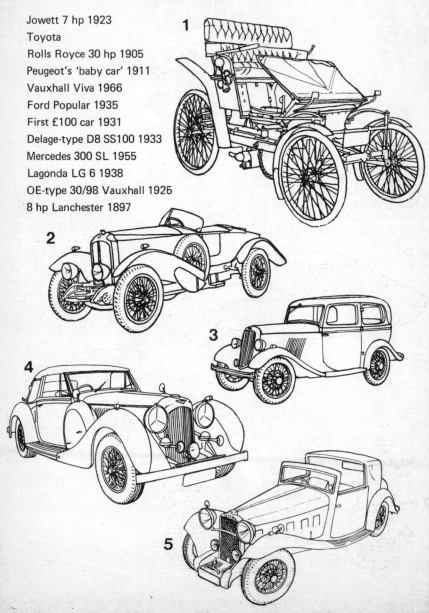

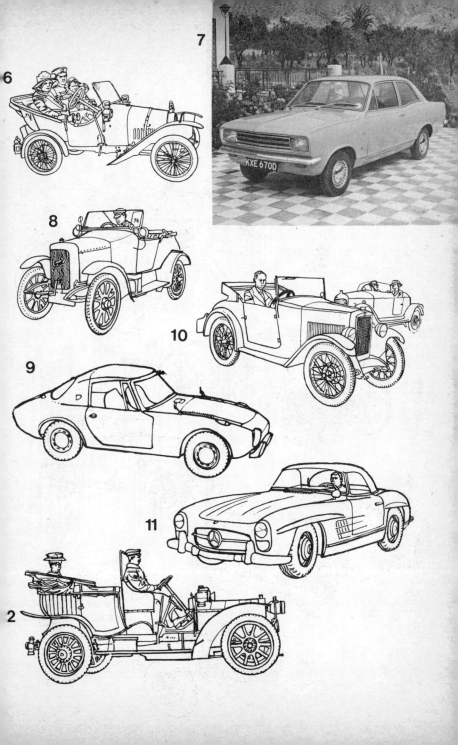

6

7

8

10

9

11

2

KXE 670D

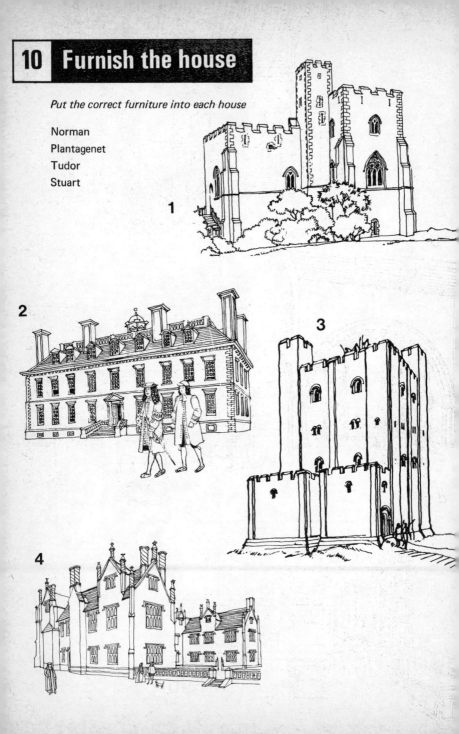

10 Furnish the house

Put the correct furniture into each house

Norman
Plantagenet
Tudor
Stuart

1

2

3

4

Whose signature?

Here are the signatures of some famous people.
Match each to one of the activities below

Playwright
Artist
Monarch
Soldier
Statesman
Novelist (author of 'Sketches by Boz')
Art critic
Poet
Composer (of 'Dream of Gerontius')
Surgeon
Novelist (author of 'Tess of the d'Urbervilles')
Lexicographer
Sailor
Scientist
Composer (of 'Fidelio')

1 *Picasso*

2 *Elizabeth R*

3 *A Einstein*

4 *Robert Burns*

5 *John Ruskin*

6 *Fra: Drake*

7 *Joseph Lister*

8

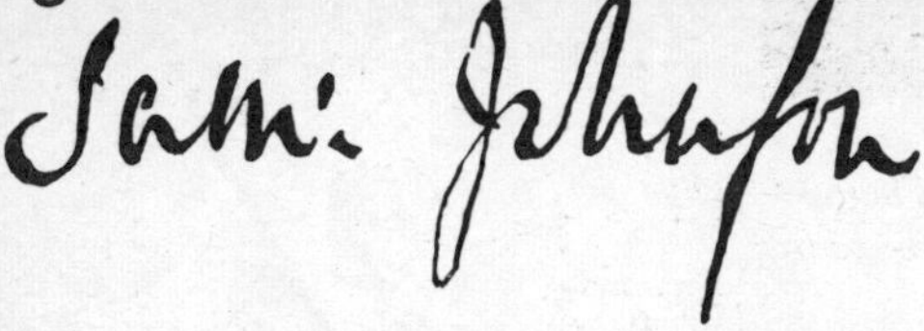

Sam: Johnson

9

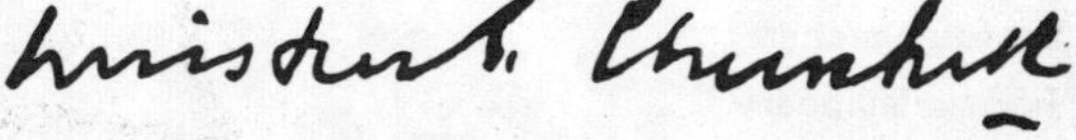

Winstant. Churchill

10

Thomas Hardy.

11

William Shakespeare

12

Charles Dickens

13

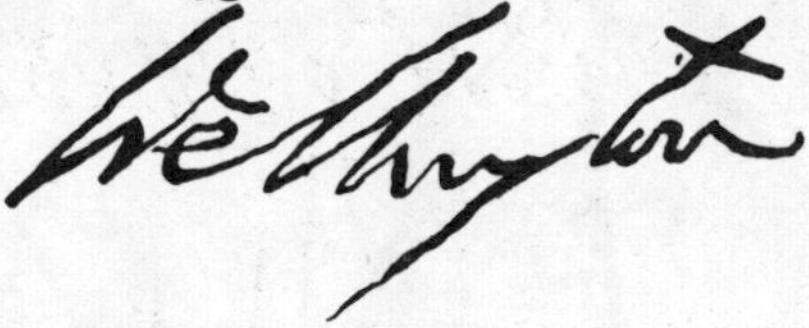

Wellington

14

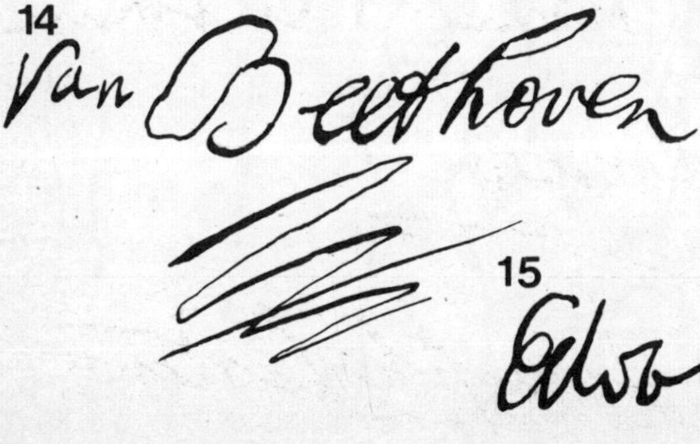

Van Beethoven

15

Edward Elgar

12 Warriors

Match the pictures to the names below

Egyptian archer
Assyrian archer
Scythian archer
Roman legionary
Norman knight
Mediaeval knight
Tudor knight
Musketeer (17th century)
French trooper (17th century)
British grenadier

13 It goes on rails

Match the pictures to the names below

The 'Novelty' 1829
Stephenson's 'Locomotion' 1825
'Hector' long boiler locomotive 1845
'Blue Belle' Caledonian railway
   racer 1886
USA 'Admiral' 1868
French 'Baltic' 1911
Pneumatic-tyred train, Paris Metro
German monorail 1909
Romney Hythe and Dymchurch
   Railway
Petrol railcar, County Donegal
   Railway, Ireland

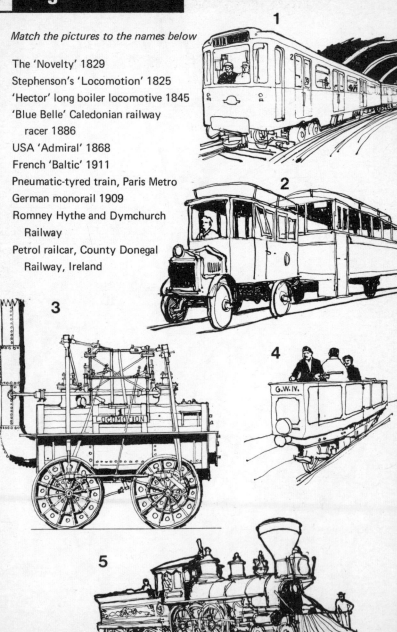

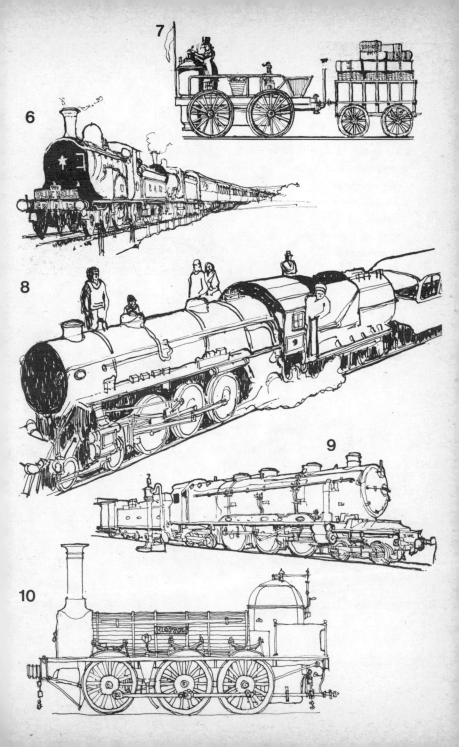

14 Birds

Match the pictures to the names below

Tawny owl
Lapwing
Partridge
Yellowhammer
Golden eagle
Skylark
Wood pigeon
Long-tailed tit
Shag
Oystercatcher
Pheasant
Hawfinch
Mallard
Sparrowhawk

15 Famous castles

Match the names and the pictures of these famous castles

Conway Castle
Tower of London
Windsor Castle
Warwick Castle
Carisbrooke Castle
Caernarvon Castle
Beaumaris Castle

1

2

3

4

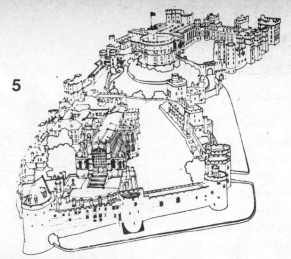

5

6

7

Match the pictures with the names below

Pilgrim in Chaucer's time
Mediaeval baggage cart
Elizabethan litter
Stage coach
Coach and four 1675
Pack mules
Irish state coach
Sedan chair
Hansom cab
Steam car 1899
Boneshaker
Elizabethan coach

1

2

3

4

5

6

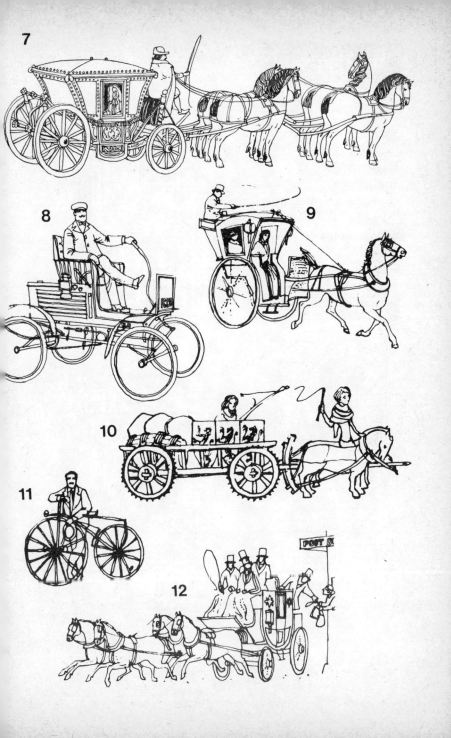

Match the pictures to the periods given below

Egyptian
Mediaeval
Tudor
Elizabethan
Early Stuart
Late Stuart
Mid-20th century
Victorian
Georgian

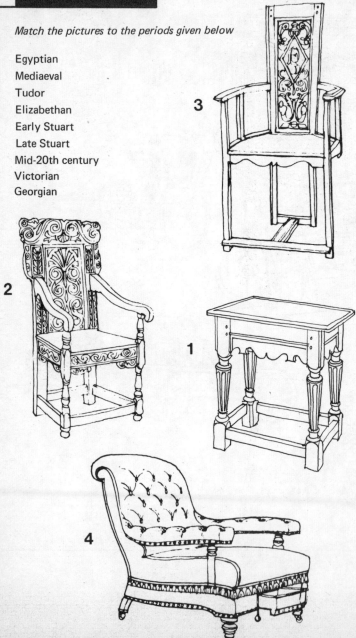

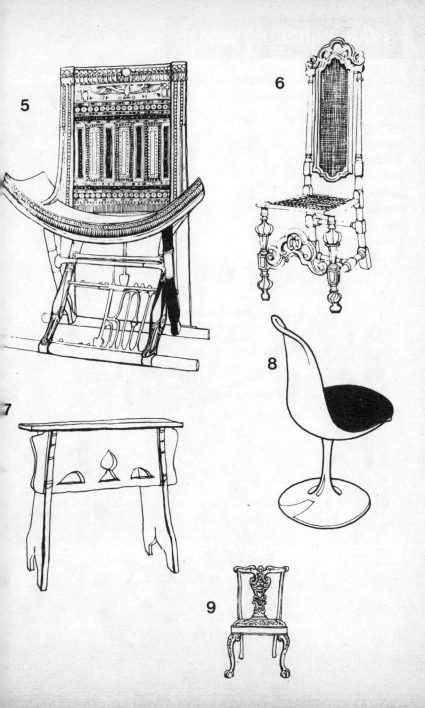

5

6

7

8

9

18 Who pioneered what?

*Which of the pioneers listed below is associated
with each invention or discovery?*

Henri Giffard
Elias Howe
Igor Sikorsky
Christopher Cockerell
Guglielmo Marconi
Karl Benz
Christopher Latham Sholes
Ambrose Fleming
George Stephenson

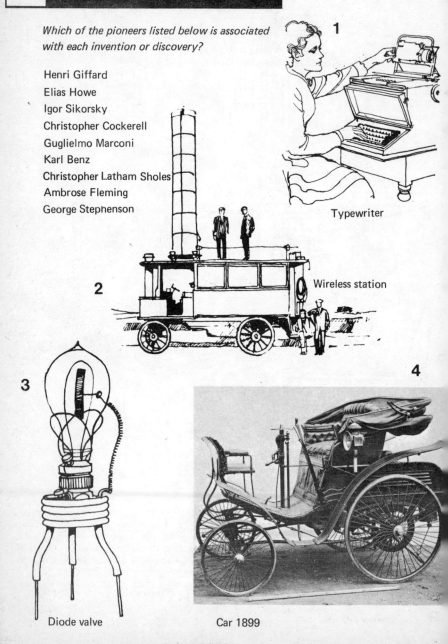

1

Typewriter

2

Wireless station

3

Diode valve

4

Car 1899

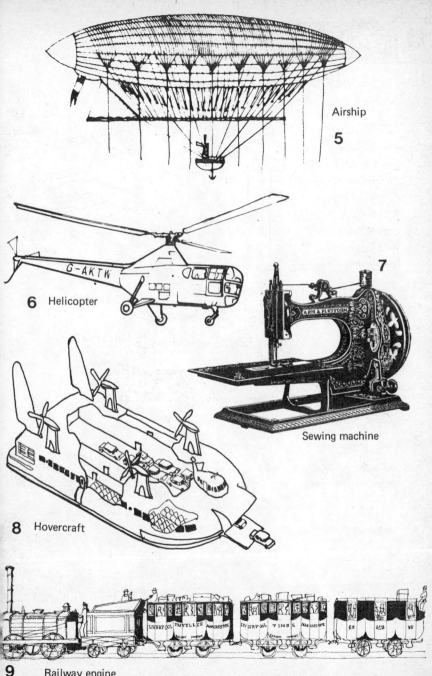

Airship

5

6 Helicopter

G-AKTW

7

Sewing machine

8 Hovercraft

9 Railway engine

*Match each of these bones to one of the labels
on the diagram*

Patella
Sternum
Scapula
Metatarsal
Fibula
Radius
Cranium
Ulna
Cervical vertebrae
Femur
Ilium
Humerus
Tibia
Clavicle

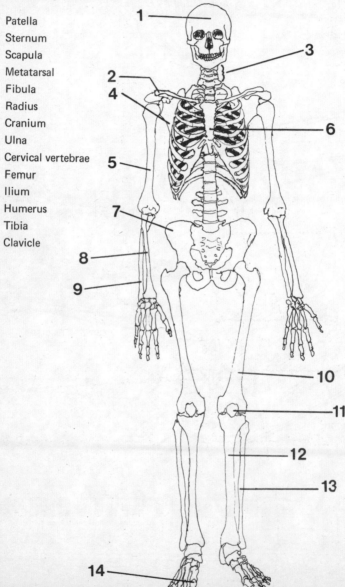

*Match each of these parts of the human body
to one of the labels on the diagram*

Heart
Lung
Oesophagus
Large intestine
Small intestine
Stomach
Pancreas
Cerebrum
Kidney
Liver

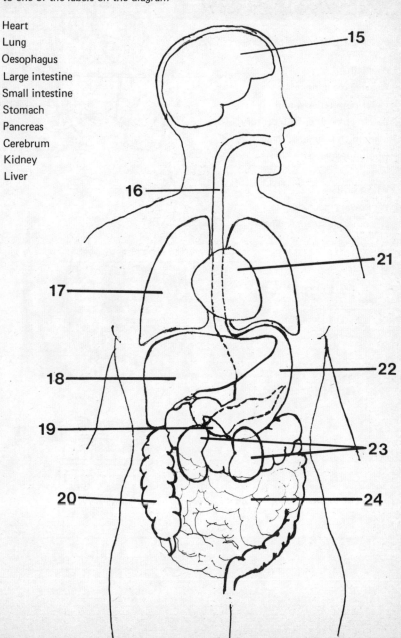

Match the pictures to the names below

Pole lathe
Weaving machine
Water-powered saw-mill
Bathing machine, 18th century
Spinning machine, 18th century
Guillotine lock gates
Plough
Wheat drill
Winnowing machine
Newcomen's steam engine

2

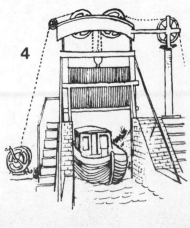

3

4

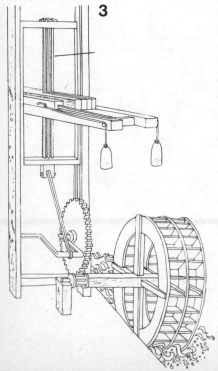

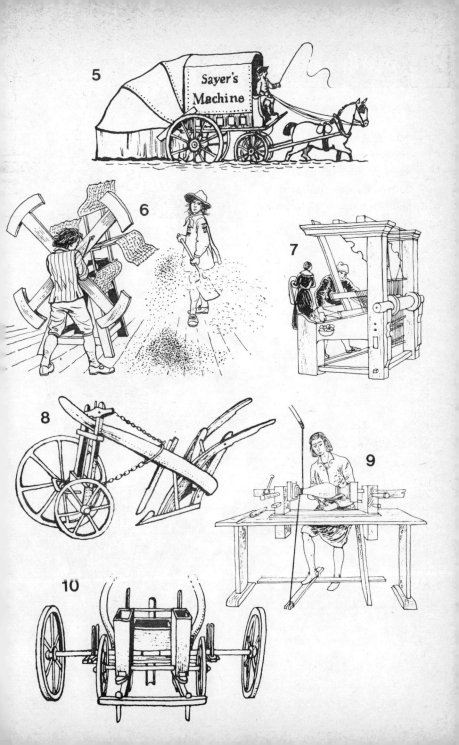

5

6

7

8

9

10

Sayer's Machine

21 Shells

Match the pictures to the names below

Chiton
Olive shell
Keyhole limpet
Tusk–shell
Cowrie
Periwinkle
Scallop
Butterfly shell
Cockle
Hard-shell clam
Button shell
Whelk
Topshell
Common mussel
Spindle shell
Lightening shell

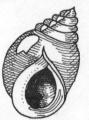

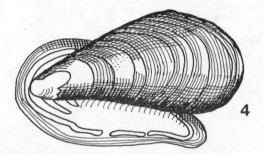

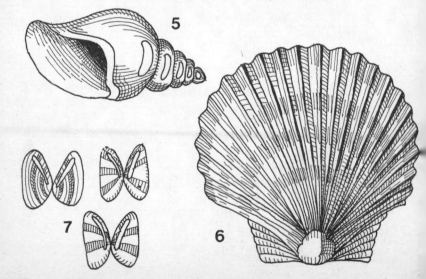

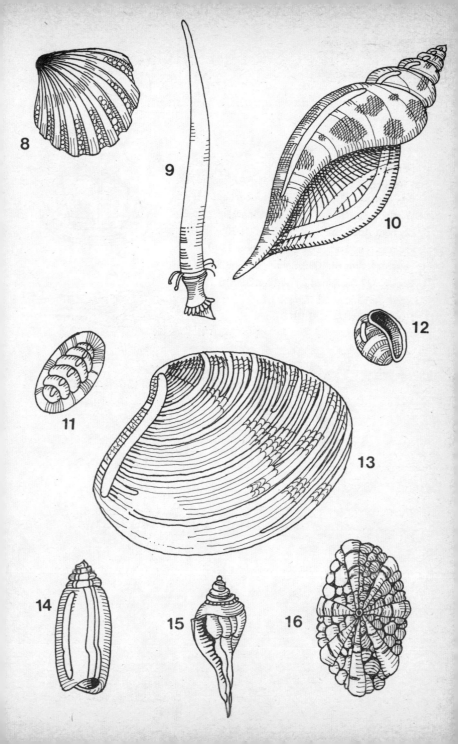

Match the pictures of these old and new planes to the names given below

BAC VC 10, jet transport
Hawker 'Hart' (1930-39) bomber
Supermarine 'Spitfire' (1938-51) RAF fighter
BAC/Breguet 'Jaguar' (1970s) support aircraft
Westland-Sud 'Puma' (1970s) helicopter
Clement Ader's monoplane 'Eole' 1890
Francesco de Lana's balloon machine 1670
Messerschmidt Bf 109E fighter, Second World War
Boeing 727 3-engined jet airliner (1970s)
North American 'Mustang' P-51
Handley-Page V/1500 1918 bomber

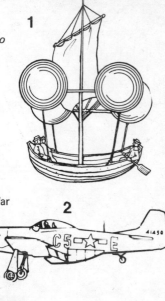

1

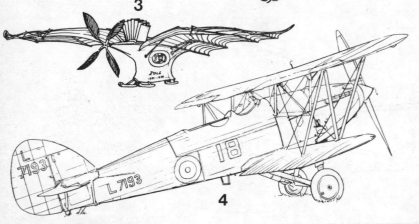

2

3

4

5

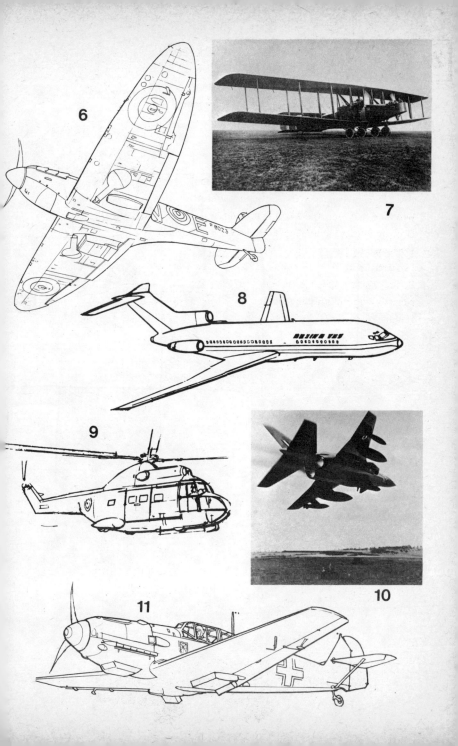

6

7

8

9

10

11

Match each of these states to one of the shaded areas on the map

Georgia   Ohio   Tennessee
New Mexico   Virginia   Minnesota
California   Pennsylvania   Nebraska
Utah   Illinois   Arkansas
Oklahoma   Wyoming

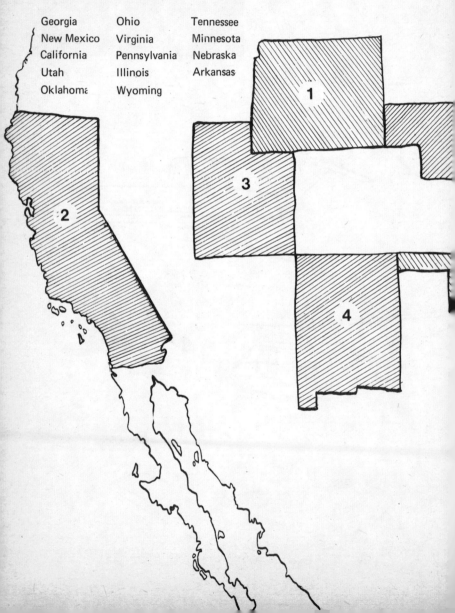

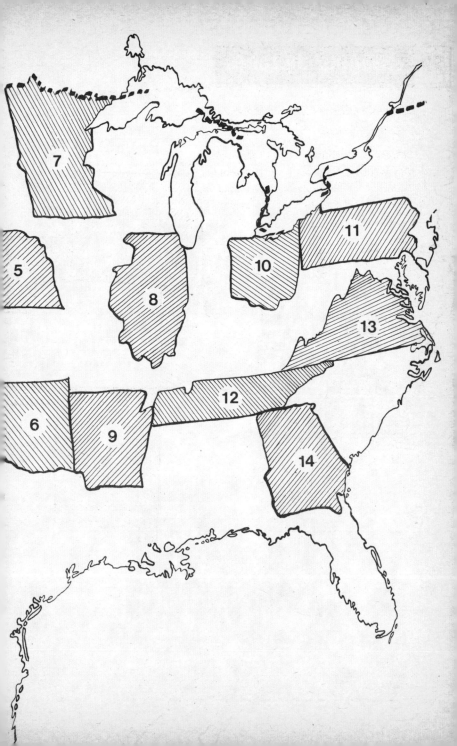

24 Famous churches

Match the pictures to the names below

St Paul's Cathedral
St George's Chapel
Westminster Abbey
St Basil's Cathedral
Wells Cathedral

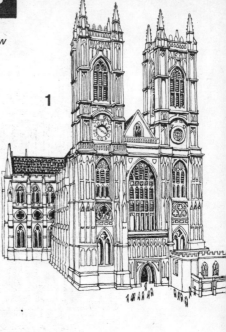

1

2

3

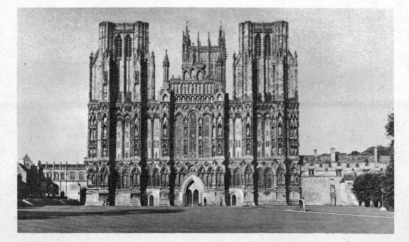

25 Museum pieces

These are unusual articles rarely used today, and
found only in museums and antique shops. Match
the pictures to their names or descriptions below

Fire engine
Well drag for recovering lost buckets
Ship anchor
Morse apparatus
Spinning wheel
Victorian telephone
Astonomical compendium
Victorian table lamp
Victorian car horn
Early marine telescope
Bone writing tablet (Saxon)
Crossbow
Hornbook (Elizabethan)

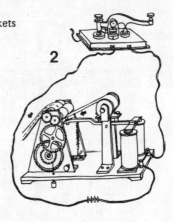

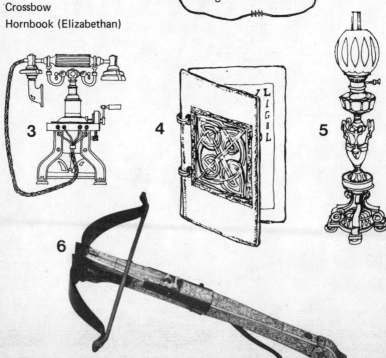

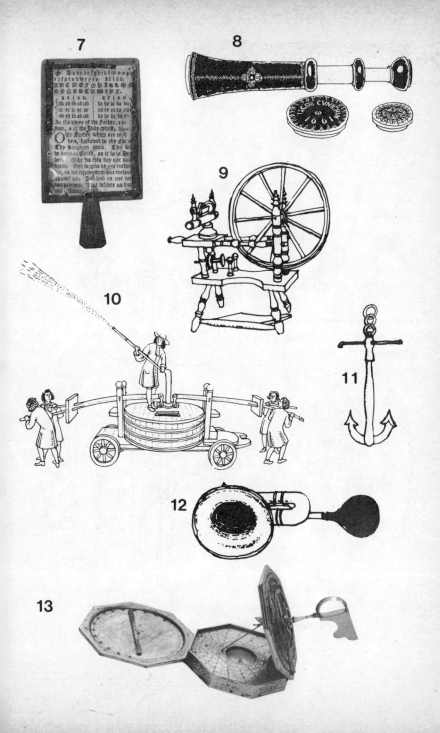

What are these people doing, or what names are given to their occupations?

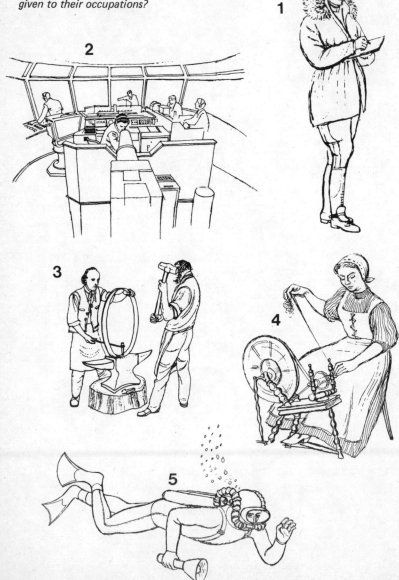

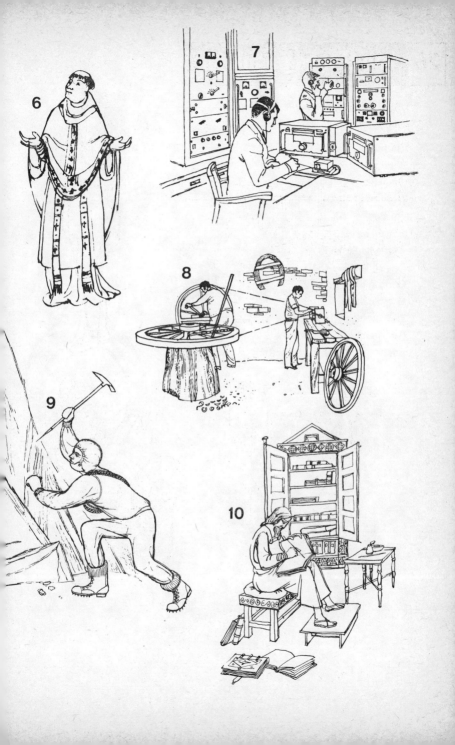

27 Helmets

Match the pictures to the names below

Etruscan c. 700 BC
Germanic 70–600 AD
Viking
Frankish c. 450 AD
Norman c. 1000–1100
Russian c. 1100
Bascinet c. 1430
Kettle-hat c. 1480
French lancer's 1810
German dragoon's 1870
Greek c. 450 BC
Pikeman's pot 1650
Roman
Embossed French 16th century

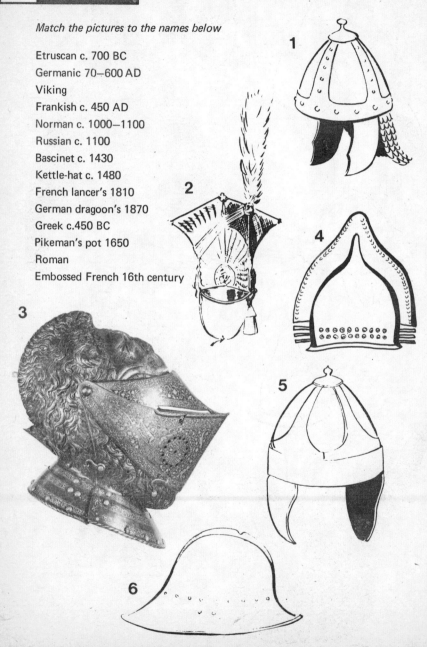

1

2

3

4

5

6

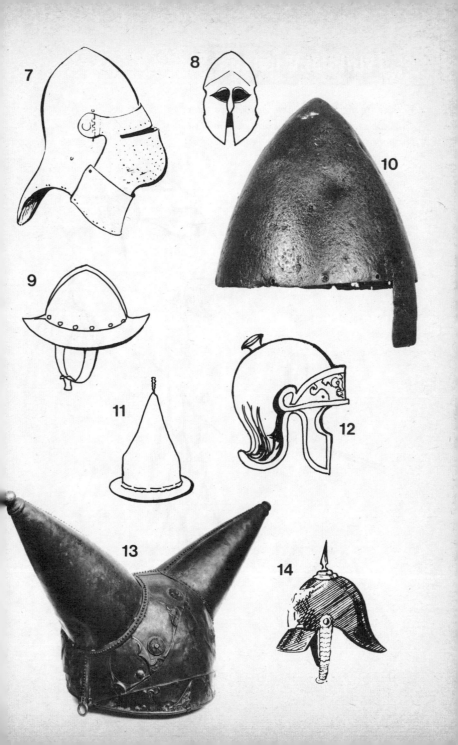

28 | Fruits and leaves

Here are the fruits of some well-known trees. Match each fruit with the corresponding leaf opposite

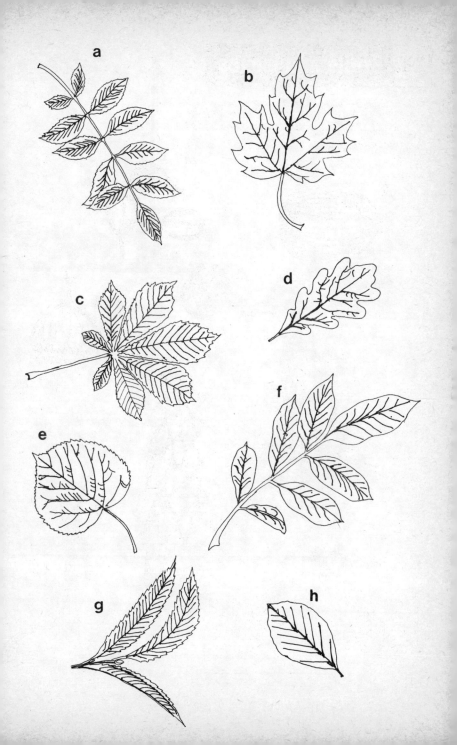

29 Ships

Match the pictures to the names below

Tortora reed boat
Polynesian double canoe
French galley   1690
Chinese junk
Canja (Nile boat)
Steam tug 1802
Cruiser 1911
Submarine
Clipper
Battleship
Battle cruiser

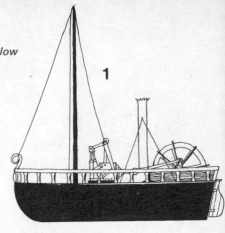

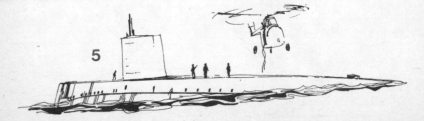

Can you tell the story behind each of these
pictures? The names of the characters may help
you

The Burghers of Calais

Richard the Lionheart

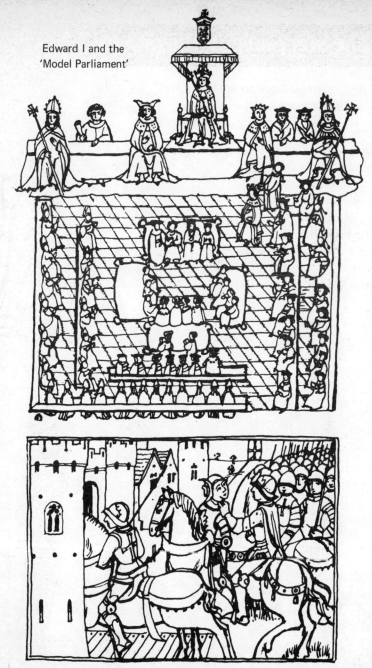

Edward I and the 'Model Parliament'

Joan of Arc

Which of the costumes might you have seen at each of these events?

Festival of Britain
Peasants' Revolt
Signing of Magna Carta
Great Fire of London
Norman invasion
Wars of the Roses
Great Exhibition
Independence of American colonies
Sailing of the Armada
Queen Victoria's Diamond Jubilee

*Match each of these parts to one of the labels on
the diagram*

Distributor   Battery   Rear axle
Gear box   Oil filter   Handbrake rods
Drive shaft   Steering column   Radiator
Drum brake   Disc brake   Air filter
Petrol tank   Sump   Trafficator
Shock absorber Silencer   Leaf springs

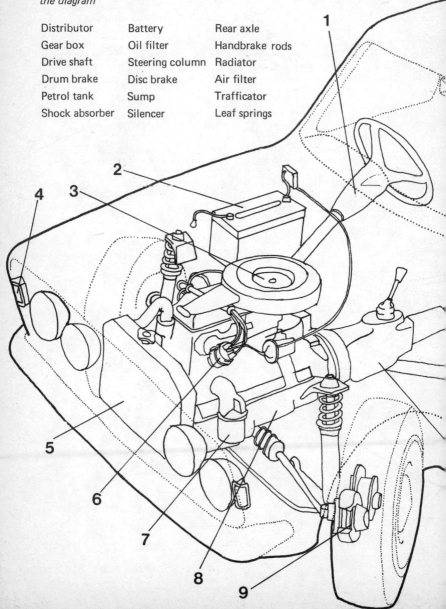

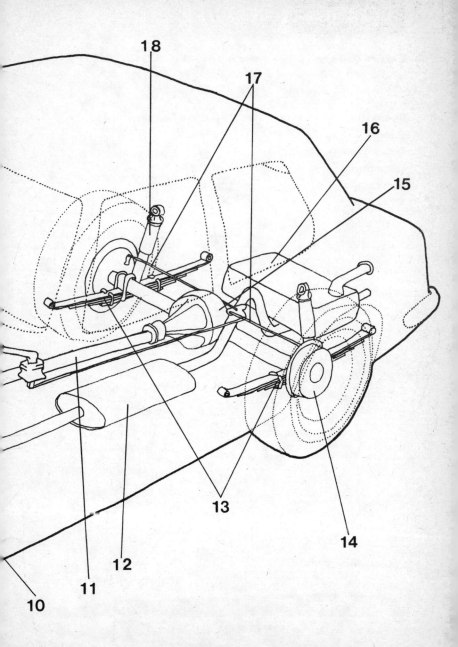

What are the sources of power that make these
vehicles or machines work?
Match one of these to each picture

Electricity
Gas
Manual (horse, ox or man)
Oil or petrol
Coal or coke
Water or wind

1

2

3

4

5

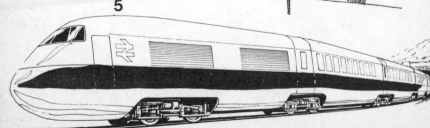

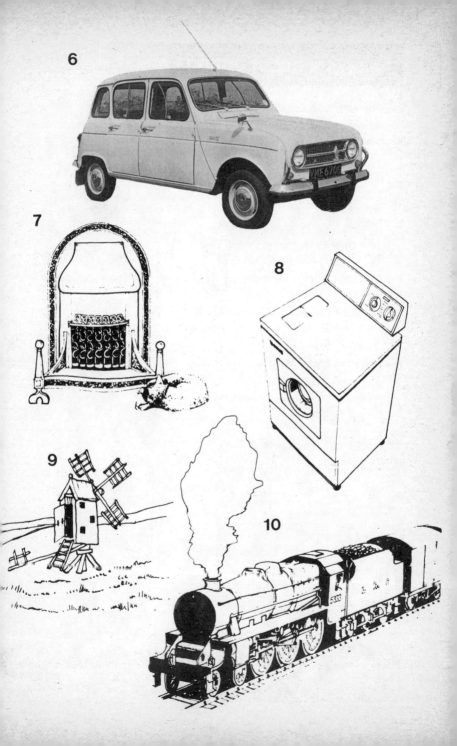

6

7

8

9

10

34 Who are these famous men?

1 Who developed a machine that used oil as fuel?
2 Who sailed round the world in 'Gypsy Moth IV'?
3 Who built ships and railways?
4 Who developed the first mass-produced motor car?
5 Who was the playwright who was also the architect of Blenheim Palace?
6 Who was the playwright, author of 'Marriage-à-la-Mode', and Poet Laureate from 1668—88?
7 Who wrote the 'Gallic War'?
8 Who is remembered for his development of a canal system?
9 Who was a Regency dandy?
10 Who was the architect and interior designer known for his designs of ceilings and fireplaces?

Sir Francis Chichester

John Vanbrugh

Dr Rudolf Diesel

Duke of Bridgewater

Henry Ford

Beau Brummel

Isambard Kingdom Brunel

Julius Caesar

John Dryden

Robert Adam

35 Spot the symbol

Here are some well-known symbols. Match each one to its correct subject below.

Electronics   Cartography   Phonetics
Mathematics   Shipping   Freemasonry
Religion   Publishing   Astronomy
Biology   Sport   Commerce
Typography   Shorthand   Currency
Music

1

2

3

4

5

6

7

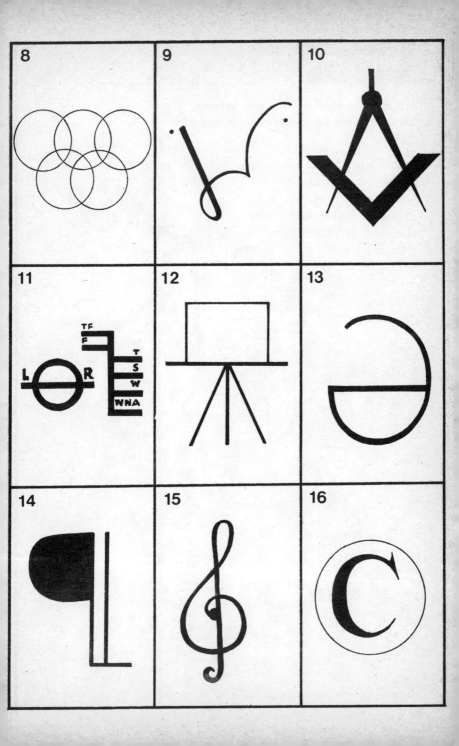

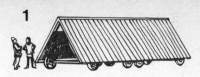

These machines and weapons were used for besieging castles. Match the pictures to the names below

Battering ram	Siege tower
Ballista	Catapult
Mangonel	Bombard
Trebuchet	Roman testudo
Penthouse	Carroballista
Pluteus	

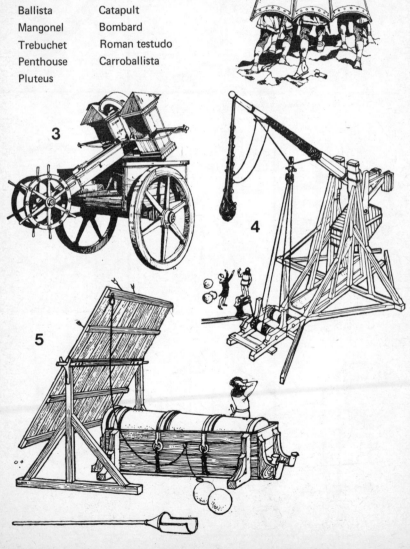

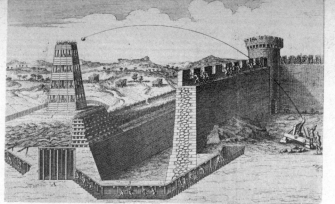

6

7

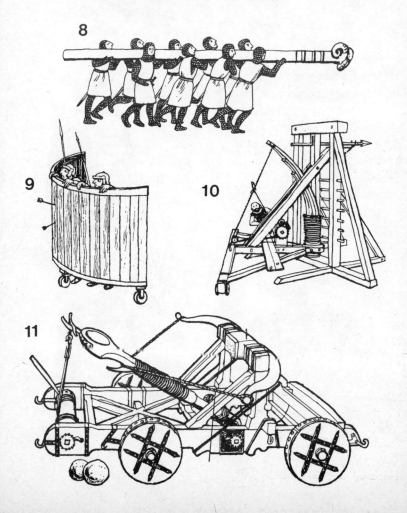

8

9

10

11

1   Who was king when Thomas à Becket was Archbishop of Canterbury?

2   Who was known as the 'Hammer of the Scots'?

3   Who was the first English Prince of Wales?

4   Who was the first king of the House of Lancaster?

5   Who led the English army in the battle of Agincourt?

6   Who held both the English and the French thrones before he was a year old?

7   Who was the popular king whose horses won the Derby three times?

8   Who was the first Norse ruler of England to be accepted as a Christian king?

9   Who was the king who fought William at the battle of Hastings?

10   Who defeated a coalition of Danes, Irish and Scots at the battle of Brunanburgh?

11   Who was the last Stuart monarch?

12   Who reigned for only nine days?

Edward VII

Edward II

Edward I

Henry Vi

Harold

Henry IV

Athelstan

Anne

Henry V

Jane Grey

Canute

Henry II

What are the stories illustrated by these pictures

Coronation, June 1953

Ceremony of the Order of the Garter

Maundy service

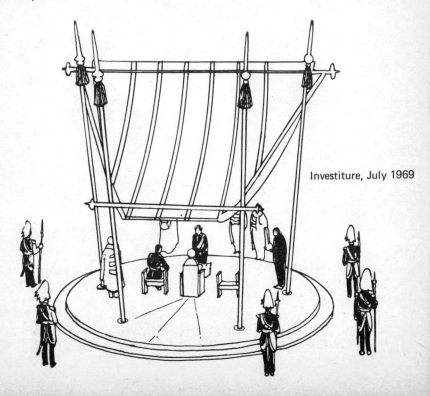

Investiture, July 1969

1 At the fishmonger's

1	Shrimp	5	Eel	9	Red mullet
2	Crab	6	Herring	10	Lobster
3	Salmon	7	Cod	11	Halibut
4	Plaice	8	Whiting	12	Pilchard

2 Coins

1	Turkey	6	Portugal	10	Lebanon
2	Italy	7	Switzerland	11	Germany
3	The Netherlands	8	Manchuria	12	Denmark
4	Ireland	9	Luxembourg	13	Greece
5	France				

3 Homes

1	Mongolian felt yurt tent	6	West African stilt house
2	Norwegian log house	7	Wood and plaster house, Cheshire
3	Siberian tent	8	Bedouin Arab tent
4	Roman villa	9	Queen Anne house
5	Chinese house	10	French château

4 Headgear

1	Miss Late Stuart	7	Miss Tudor
2	Miss Roman Empire	8	Miss Georgian
3	Miss Ancient Egypt	9	Miss Norman
4	Miss White and Red Rose	10	Miss Late Victorian
5	Miss Early Stuart	11	Miss Elizabeth I
6	Miss Early Victorian		

5 Cavalry

1 Saxon c. 700 AD
2 Assyrian c. 700 BC
3 British dragoon c. 1815
4 Parthian c. 50 BC
5 Italian c. 1325

6 English lancer c. 1850
7 German c. 1480
8 Japanese c. 1600
9 British carabineer c. 1600
10 Gothic c. 500 AD

6 Postmarks

1 Austria
2 Iran
3 East Germany (Leipzig)
4 South Africa
5 Spain

6 West Germany (Frankfurt am Main)
7 Sweden
8 Ireland
9 Poland

7 Countries and counties

1 Norway
2 Finland
3 Poland
4 Belgium
5 Switzerland
6 Hungary
7 Italy
8 Albania

9 Bulgaria
10 Denmark
11 Cumbria
12 Tyne and Wear
13 Cleveland
14 Humberside
15 Nottinghamshire
16 West Midlands

17 Dyfed
18 Gwent
19 Avon
20 Buckinghamshire
21 Cambridgeshire
22 Devon
23 Hampshire
24 Kent

8 Old London

1 Vauxhall Gardens 1765
2 Royal Exchange before the Great Fire
3 St Bride's Church, by Wren

4 Theatre Royal, Drury Lane
5 St George's, Hanover Square
6 Great Piazza, Covent Garden

9 | It goes on wheels

1	8 hp Lanchester 1897	7	Vauxhall Viva 1966
2	OE-type 30/98 Vauxhall 1925	8	Jowett 7 hp 1923
3	Ford Popular 1935	9	Toyota
4	Lagonda LG 6 1938	10	First £100 car 1931
5	Delage-type D8 SS100 1933	11	Mercedes 300 SL 1955
6	Peugeot's 'baby car' 1911	12	Rolls Royce 30 hp 1905

10 | Furnish the house

1a Plantagenet   2d Stuart   3b Norman   4c Tudor

11 | Whose signature?

1	Artist (Picasso)	11	Playwright (William Shakespeare)
2	Monarch (Elizabeth I)	12	Novelist (author of 'Sketches by Boz') (Charles Dickens)
3	Scientist (Albert Einstein)	13	Soldier (Duke of Wellington)
4	Poet (Robert Burns)	14	Composer (of 'Fidelio') (Ludwig von Beethoven)
5	Art critic (John Ruskin)	15	Composer (of 'Dream of Gerontius') (Sir Edward Elgar)
6	Sailor (Francis Drake)		
7	Surgeon (Joseph Lister)		
8	Lexicographer (Samuel Johnson)		
9	Statesman (Sir Winston Churchill)		
10	Novelist (author of 'Tess of the d'Urbervilles') (Thomas Hardy)		

12 | Warriors

1	British grenadier	6	Scythian archer
2	Mediaeval knight	7	Assyrian archer
3	Norman knight	8	French trooper (17th century)
4	Tudor knight	9	Roman legionary
5	Egyptian archer	10	Musketeer (17th century)

13 It goes on rails

1 Pneumatic-tyred train, Paris metro
2 Petrol railcar, County Donegal Railway, Ireland
3 Stephenson's 'Locomotion' 1825
4 German monorail 1909
5 USA 'Admiral' 1868
6 'Blue Belle' Caledonian railway racer 1886
7 The 'Novelty' 1829
8 Romney Hythe and Dymchurch Railway
9 French 'Baltic' 1911
10 'Hector' long boiler locomotive 1845

14 Birds

1 Hawfinch
2 Shag
3 Wood pigeon
4 Sparrowhawk
5 Pheasant
6 Mallard
7 Lapwing
8 Skylark
9 Tawny Owl
10 Long-tailed tit
11 Golden eagle
12 Oystercatcher
13 Yellowhammer
14 Partridge

15 Famous castles

1 Warwick Castle
2 Tower of London
3 Carisbrooke Castle
4 Caernarvon Castle
5 Windsor Castle
6 Beaumaris Castle
7 Conway Castle

16 On the road

1 Pack mules
2 Elizabethan litter
3 Elizabethan coach
4 Pilgrim in Chaucer's time
5 Sedan chair
6 Irish state coach
7 Coach and four 1675
8 Steam car 1899
9 Hansom cab
10 Mediaeval baggage cart
11 Boneshaker
12 Stage coach

17 Take a chair

1	Elizabethan	6	Late Stuart
2	Early Stuart	7	Mediaeval
3	Tudor	8	Mid-20th century
4	Victorian	9	Georgian
5	Egyptian		

18 Who pioneered what?

1	Christopher Latham Sholes	6	Igor Sikorsky
2	Guglielmo Marconi	7	Elias Howe
3	Ambrose Fleming	8	Christopher Cockerell
4	Karl Benz	9	George Stephenson
5	Henri Giffard		

19 The human body

1	Cranium	9	Ulna	17	Lung
2	Clavicle	10	Femur	18	Liver
3	Cervical vertebrae	11	Patella	19	Pancreas
4	Scapula	12	Tibia	20	Large intestine
5	Humerus	13	Fibula	21	Heart
6	Sternum	14	Metatarsal	22	Stomach
7	Ilium	15	Cerebrum	23	Kidney
8	Radius	16	Oesophagus	24	Small intestine

20 Historical machines

1	Spinning machine, 18th century	6	Winnowing machine
2	Newcomen's steam engine	7	Weaving machine
3	Water-powered saw-mill	8	Plough
4	Guillotine lock gates	9	Pole lathe
5	Bathing machine, 18th century	10	Wheat drill

21 Shells

1	Cowrie	7	Butterfly shell	12	Button shell
2	Topshell	8	Cockle	13	Hard-shell clam
3	Periwinkle	9	Tusk-shell	14	Olive shell
4	Common mussel	10	Spindle shell	15	Lightening shell
5	Whelk	11	Chiton	16	Keyhole limpet
6	Scallop				

22 Aviation

1 Francesco de Lana's balloon machine 1670
2 North American 'Mustang' P-51
3 Clement Ader's monoplane 'Eole' 1890
4 Hawker 'Hart' (1930-39) bomber
5 BAC VC 10, jet transport
6 Supermarine 'Spitfire' (1938-51) RAF fighter
7 Handley-Page V/1500 1918 bomber
8 Boeing 727 3-engined jet airliner (1970s)
9 Westland-Sud 'Puma' (1970s) helicopter
10 BAC/Breguet 'Jaguar' (1970s) support aircraft
11 Messerschmidt Bf 109E fighter, Second World War

23 States of America

1	Wyoming	5	Nebraska	9	Arkansas	13	Virginia
2	California	6	Oklahoma	10	Ohio	14	Georgia
3	Utah	7	Minnesota	11	Pennsylvania		
4	New Mexico	8	Illinois	12	Tennessee		

24 Famous churches

1	Westminster Abbey	4	St Paul's Cathedral
2	St Basil's Cathedral (Moscow)	5	St. George's Chapel (Windsor)
3	Wells Cathedral		

25 Museum pieces

1   Well drag for recovering lost buckets
2   Morse apparatus
3   Victorian telephone
4   Bone writing tablet (Saxon)
5   Victorian table lamp
6   Cross bow
7   Hornbook (Elizabethan)
8   Early marine telescope
9   Spinning wheel
10 Fire engine
11 Ship anchor
12 Victorian car horn
13 Astronomical compendium

26 The things people do

1   Canadian mountie
2   Air traffic controllers (airports)
3   Blacksmith
4   Spinner, 19th century
5   Frogman
6   Priest
7   Radio operator (on board ship)
8   Wheelwright
9   Mountaineer
10 Scribe

27 Helmets

1   Germanic 70-600 AD
2   French lancer's 1810
3   Embossed French 16th century
4   Etruscan c. 700 BC
5   Frankish c. 450 AD
6   Kettle-hat c. 1480
7   Bascinet c. 1430
8   Greek c. 450 BC
9   Pikeman's pot 1650
10 Norman c. 1000-1100
11 Russian c. 1100
12 Roman
13 Viking
14 German dragoon's 1870

28 Fruits and leaves

1   h (beech)
2   f (walnut)
3   c (horse chestnut)
4   g (chestnut)
5   d (oak)
6   a (ash)
7   b (plane)
8   e (linden)

29 Ships

1	Steam tug 1802	5	Submarine	9	Polynesian double canoe
2	Clipper	6	Battleship	10	Cruiser 1911
3	Canja (Nile boat)	7	French galley 1690	11	Tortora reed boat
4	Battle cruiser	8	Chinese junk		

30 The story behind the picture I

The Burghers of Calais — heroically offered to sacrifice themselves to help their fellow-citizens when the city was besieged by Edward III in 1347 after the battle of Crecy.

Edward I and the 'Model Parliament' — 'Model Parliament' is the name given to the assembly which met in 1295 in order to grant money to Edward I for his wars against France and Scotland. It was the first time that citizens and burgesses were represented as well as the nobility and so is considered the model for future Parliaments.

Richard the Lionheart — was seized by Leopold, Duke of Austria in his journey home after a crusade to the Holy Land in 1192. It is said that his minstrel, Blondel, discovered the castle in which he was held a prisoner before he was released on ransom.

Joan of Arc — was a peasant girl who dressed in armour and led the French against the English in the Hundred Years' War. The picture shows her as a prisoner at Compiegne, where she was taken in 1430. She was condemned as a witch and burnt at the stake.

31 Dressed for the occasion

1	Queen Victoria's Diamond Jubilee, 1897	5	Wars of the Roses, 1455-1485
2	Peasants' Revolt, 1381	6	Festival of Britain, 1951
3	Norman invasion, 1066	7	Great Exhibition, 1851
4	Independence of American colonies, 1776-1783	8	Signing of Magna Carta, 1215
		9	Great Fire of London, 1666
		10	Sailing of the Armada, 1588

32 Car parts

1	Steering column	6	Distributor	11	Drive shaft	15	Rear axle
2	Battery	7	Oil filter	12	Silencer	16	Petrol tank
3	Air filter	8	Sump	13	Leaf springs	17	Handbrake rods
4	Trafficator	9	Disc brake	14	Drum brake	18	Shock absorber
5	Radiator	10	Gear box				

33 What makes it work?

1	Water or wind (yacht)	6	Oil or petrol
2	Gas (Victorian street lamp)	7	Gas (Victorian household fire)
3	Manual (organ)	8	Electricity (washing machine)
4	Manual (church bell)	9	Water or wind (mill)
5	Electricity (Advanced Passenger Train)	10	Coal or coke (steam train)

34 Who are these famous men?

1	Dr Rudolf Diesel	4	Henry Ford	7	Julius Caesar
2	Sir Francis Chichester	5	John Vanburgh	8	Duke of Bridgewater
3	Isambard Kingdom Brunel	6	John Dryden	9	Beau Brummel
				10	Robert Adam

35 Spot the symbol

1	Cartography (scene of battle)	9	Shorthand
2	Religion (chi-rho sign)	10	Freemasonry
3	Currency (lire)	11	Shipping (Plimsoll line)
4	Commerce (at)	12	Electronics (transistor)
5	Mathematics (square root)	13	Phonetics (schwa)
6	Astronomy (Uranus)	14	Typography (paragraph mark)
7	Biology (Hermaphrodite)	15	Music (treble clef)
8	Sport (Olympic Games)	16	Publishing (copyright mark)

36 Weapons

1	Penthouse	4	Trebuchet	7	Catapult	10	Ballista
2	Roman testudo	5	Bombard	8	Battering ram	11	Mangonel
3	Carroballista	6	Siege tower	9	Pluteus		

37 Kings and Queens

1	Henry II	4	Henry IV	7	Edward VII	10	Athelstan
2	Edward I	5	Henry V	8	Canute	11	Anne
3	Edward II	6	Henry VI	9	Harold	12	Jane Grey

38 The story behind the picture II

Coronation, June 1953 — the ceremony in which the new sovereign, Queen Elizabeth II, was invested with the symbols of the authority and responsibility of monarchy. In England, the ceremony always takes place in Westminster Abbey and is surrounded by ritual, often mediaeval in origin.

Ceremony of the Order of the Garter. The Order of the Garter is the highest order of English chivalry and was instituted by Edward III on St George's Day in 1348. The Motto is 'Honi soi qui mal y pense' — 'Evil to him who evil thinks'. Each year a service is held at Windsor Castle attended by all the Knights in their regalia.

Maundy service. This is connected with Jesus's washing of the disciples' feet at the Last Supper and his command that they should do likewise. Now there is a special service on the eve of Good Friday at which the sovereign presents specially minted coins to one man and one woman for each year of the sovereign's age.

Investiture, July 1969. This is a ceremony in which the heir apparent, the eldest son of the reigning monarch, is officially invested with the title of Prince of Wales and he in turn promises loyalty to his sovereign. The title was first bestowed on Prince Edward, later Edward II, in 1284. Prince Charles was invested at Caernarvon and was then presented to the Welsh people.

Much of the illustrative material incorporated into the Picture Quiz Books is drawn from the large and growing series of Picture Reference Books of which Boswell Taylor is also the General Editor. This series is designed to provide authentic and accurate background material and therefore may form a useful reference library. Most illustrations are taken from original sources.

Here is a complete list of titles so far available:

JONATHAN

I'd get married in a minute if I found the right girl.

SANDY

Bullshit artist! You and your actress friends.

JONATHAN

Are you kidding, Doctor? You're the one with the deal. I mean, what can I say? Take off your clothes, baby, I'm gonna check out your capital gains?

SANDY

I just look.

JONATHAN

Sure you do.

SANDY

I really do. Susan's plenty enough woman for one man. Hey, will you look at that?

JONATHAN

That's Sally Joyce.

SANDY

Didn't I see her on Ed Sullivan?

JONATHAN

I fucked her once.

SANDY

Bullshit artist!

JONATHAN

We used to do her taxes. She's with another firm now.

SANDY

Why don't you say hello?

She would
that one.

Yeah?

His eyes begin to

You think a
she's out f
money and
hung than t

I should hav

Listen, it's n
don't think
year now. M
This last one
A good pair
most no ass a
legs—I would
more inches
more inches
took two year

You don't wa

I don't want t

You can

(Annoy
You're

Interior: Jon
Close-up: San

Susan'
home,
cause
then
nice
home
much
other
we d
we n
or co
not

Shot: Jona

Close-up: Sandy

> **SANDY**
>
> There are other things besides glamour.

Cut to:

Interior: the Rainbow Room

Shot: A dinner table over which BOBBIE's hand holds JONA-THAN's hand. The index finger of her other hand traces a line down his open palm. Behind the table we catch a view of BOBBIE's massive bosom.

> **BOBBIE**
>
> You have a long life-line.

> **JONATHAN**
>
> I like that, the way you run your nail across the in-side of my—

> **BOBBIE**
>
> You are difficult to get along with.

> **JONATHAN**
>
> Me? Bobbie!

> **BOBBIE**
>
> You always know your own mind.

> **JONATHAN**
>
> *(Leers)* Right this minute anyway.

> **BOBBIE**
>
> You won't stop going after what you want until you get it.

JONATHAN

(Smiles) Let's see your hand.

He stares at it.

BOBBIE

Well?

JONATHAN

You are built.

BOBBIE

You see that in my hand?

JONATHAN

Even your hand is built.

BOBBIE

I think you're a dirty old man.

JONATHAN

A dirty young man. How old are you?

BOBBIE

How old do you think I am?

JONATHAN

Nineteen?

BOBBIE

No.

JONATHAN

Twenty?

BOBBIE

No.

JONATHAN

Twenty-one?

BOBBIE

No.

JONATHAN

Twenty-two?

BOBBIE

No.

JONATHAN

Twenty-four?

BOBBIE

You skipped twenty-three.

JONATHAN

Twenty-three?

BOBBIE

No.

JONATHAN

Twenty-four?

BOBBIE

No.

JONATHAN

Twenty-five?

BOBBIE

No.

JONATHAN

Twenty-six?

BOBBIE

No.

JONATHAN

Twenty-seven?

You're getting warm.

JONATHAN

Twenty-eight?

BOBBIE

No.

JONATHAN

Twenty-nine?

She nods.

JONATHAN

I like going out with older women.

Cut to:

Interior: taxi—night

JONATHAN and BOBBIE sit huddled together.

BOBBIE

Are you married?

JONATHAN

Are you kidding?

BOBBIE

You don't want to get married?

JONATHAN

I'd marry you in a minute. Can you cook?

BOBBIE

Spaghetti.

JONATHAN

I can cook spaghetti.

BOBBIE

Good. Then you'll do the cooking.

JONATHAN

What'll you do?

BOBBIE

What would you like me to do?

JONATHAN

What would you like to do?

BOBBIE

I asked you first.

JONATHAN

I'm not gonna answer first.

They both laugh.

BOBBIE

I can sew.

JONATHAN

Doesn't sound like much of a marriage. Me cooking
spaghetti and you sewing.

BOBBIE

You want a divorce? I'll take you for every cent
you've got.

JONATHAN

I didn't know I was marrying a gold digger.

BOBBIE

Mm-hmmm!

She nods vigorously.

JONATHAN

You won't take pity on me?

BOBBIE

Only if you say you're sorry.

JONATHAN

I'm sorry.

BOBBIE

And you'll never do it again.

JONATHAN

I'll never do it again.

BOBBIE

And you'll always be a good boy.

JONATHAN

Yes, mama.

BOBBIE

Do you like to be mothered?

JONATHAN

I'd like to be smothered—by you.

BOBBIE

What else would you like me to do to you?

Cut to:

Interior: Jonathan's apartment—night

JONATHAN

How do you like it?

BOBBIE

How do I like what?

JONATHAN

My—you know.

BOBBIE

What do I know?

JONATHAN

You know everything.

BOBBIE

I know you.

JONATHAN

And I know you.

He sinks to his knees, buries his head in her breasts, and groans.

Cut to:

Interior: Jonathan's bedroom—night

Lights out. A little light spills from the bathroom. JONATHAN and BOBBIE in bed.

BOBBIE

(A low moan)

JONATHAN

Jesus.

BOBBIE

Baby.

JONATHAN

Jesus!

BOBBIE

Oh—baby—

JONATHAN

Oh—God—

BOBBIE

Oh—baby!

JONATHAN

Oh—God!

BOBBIE

God! God!

JONATHAN

Jesus!

BOBBIE

Baby!!

JONATHAN

Oh—Jesus!

BOBBIE

God! God!

JONATHAN

Oh baby!!

BOBBIE

Christ! God!

JONATHAN

Jesus! Jesus!

BOBBIE

Baby!! Christ!!

JONATHAN

Baby!! God!!

Babeeegodjeeeesuuuuus—

A long pause. Heavy breathing.

JONATHAN

Wow—I almost came that time.

They scream with laughter.

Cut to:

Interior: Jonathan's bedroom—day

BOBBIE is lying on the bed, on her stomach, naked. She is reading the Sunday papers, which are scattered all about. She is eating lox and bagel.

Sound: Classical music on the radio.
The shower. It stops.

JONATHAN'S VOICE

Oh, nurse.

BOBBIE

What is it, Mr. Weisenborn?

JONATHAN'S VOICE

Will you come in here for just a minute?

BOBBIE

Certainly, Mr. Weisenborn.

She hops off the bed, still eating, and enters the bathroom.

BOBBIE'S VOICE

Why, Mr. Weisenborn!

Interior: Jonathan's bedroom—night

BOBBIE and JONATHAN lie in bed, looking very comfortable with each other.

> BOBBIE
>
> Most guys I know are pricks. I don't know any more what they want.

> JONATHAN
>
> I'll be happy to tell you. *(Playful)* They want the boodle.

He slaps her ass.

> JONATHAN
>
> But they aint gonna get the boodle.

> BOBBIE
>
> Goddamn right.

> JONATHAN
>
> Because this kid here has the boodle.

> BOBBIE
>
> Pretty sure of yourself, aren't you? *(A pause)* You're a nice man.

> JONATHAN
>
> And you're a very lucky girl.

He leaves the bed and goes to the bathroom.

Sound: The shower.

BOBBIE sits up, looks thoughtful. The shower stops. JONA-THAN comes out of the bathroom.

BOBBIE

You know something, Sam?

JONATHAN

(Doing Bogart) Whad ish it, Shweedheart?

BOBBIE

You think it would be a fatal mistake in our lives if we shacked up?

JONATHAN freezes. After a moment:

JONATHAN

It's very difficult, Bobbie—these last couple of weeks —we get along so well—the idea—I like you very much, so much—this idea. To be perfectly honest—I mean, this sounds good to me— Let's both give it a couple of days to think about it— It sounds like— well, very good. Very, very—well—good. Only our eyes should be open. If we should go into this we should know exactly what we're getting into—

BOBBIE

This is just a shack-up! I'm not asking for your hand in marriage!

JONATHAN

Yeah. Well, as long as we both understand that.

BOBBIE

Well, we both do.

JONATHAN

I just thought it's better to get it all out on the table so later on there's no possibility of a misunderstanding. I don't know how many business deals I've seen come to grief because—

Okay!

JONATHAN
Okay.

BOBBIE
You're a real prick, you know that?

Cut to:

Interior: bar—day
Close-up: Jonathan

JONATHAN
I could easily get serious about this girl. She's a lot of fun to be with— *(Pause)* This is just between the two of us but for a year or so now I've been having —I don't know—a little trouble—I wasn't worried, but still and all—a little trouble with, well, myself, you know, getting hard. It took a long time and you know girls today—they judge you, they judge you very quickly. So I had some real rough times a couple of times. Some very nasty innuendoes. And as I say, I wasn't too worried, but I won't lie to you, I was a little worried. And then this Bobbie comes along and I get one look at the size of the pair on her and I never had a doubt I wouldn't be all right again. And I was. I was. With all our kidding back and forth our first night together I don't mind telling you I had tears in my eyes.

SANDY
She's really the girl in the airline commercial?

He nods.

SANDY

You lucky son of a bitch!

JONATHAN

I don't know—I don't want to get in over my head. I got in over my head three or four times already and you have to be a real bastard. I don't like being put in that position. What would you do?

SANDY

If she looks anything like she looks on television.

JONATHAN

Size 38 with a D cup.

SANDY

(Takes a deep breath) But looks aren't everything.

JONATHAN

Believe me, looks are everything.

SANDY

(Very seriously) Maybe.

Cut to:

Interior: Jonathan's bedroom—evening

JONATHAN and BOBBIE in bed.

JONATHAN

I'm hungry.

BOBBIE

I'll get up.

JONATHAN

Why do we always have to eat so late?

BOBBIE

Because I work late, dumbo.

JONATHAN

Why do you have to work at all?

BOBBIE

It brings in extra money.

JONATHAN

I make enough.

BOBBIE

You want me to quit working?

JONATHAN

I thought you were bored with it.

BOBBIE

I am.

JONATHAN

So quit.

BOBBIE

What'll I do?

JONATHAN

What do other women do?

BOBBIE

Have children.

JONATHAN leaves the bed and goes into the bathroom.

78

You asked me.

Sound: The shower.

Cut to:

Interior: Jonathan's kitchen—night

Track with BOBBIE as she removes two TV dinners from the oven, sets them up on two trays, and carries them into the bedroom. She wears a bathrobe. JONATHAN is on the bed, sitting up against the pillow. He wears an open shirt, trousers, socks. He is watching TV: an old Dick Powell musical. BOBBIE hands JONATHAN his tray.

JONATHAN

What about my beer?

BOBBIE

We're out.

JONATHAN

I really wanted a beer.

BOBBIE

Want me to run out to the corner?

JONATHAN

You're too tired.

BOBBIE

I'm tired but I don't mind.

JONATHAN

I'll get it.

No, I'll get it.

JONATHAN

It's my fault. I knew I should have reminded you when I called this afternoon.

BOBBIE

I'm sorry, honey.

JONATHAN starts to rise.

JONATHAN

You're more tired now than when you were working.

BOBBIE

I'm in the house all day.

JONATHAN

Didn't you get up at all today? What do you do? I mean, besides telephone.

BOBBIE

I'm not on the phone that much.

JONATHAN

It took me forty-five minutes to get through this afternoon. I'll go get the beer.

BOBBIE

Let me go.

JONATHAN

I thought you were too tired.

BOBBIE

I haven't been out all day.

JONATHAN

A little fresh air will do you good.

BOBBIE gets up.

A pause.

BOBBIE

Will you walk me?

JONATHAN

Then I may as well go myself.

A pause.

JONATHAN

You want to make love?

A pause.

JONATHAN

We haven't in a week.

BOBBIE

Is it a week?

Cut to:

Interior: Jonathan's living room—night

Close-up: SANDY, a cigar in his hand.

SANDY

It's funny. Susan and I do all the right things. We undress in front of each other. We spend fifteen minutes on foreplay. We experiment. Do it in different rooms. It's a seven-room house. We don't believe in making a ritual of it. We do it when we feel like it. We don't worry about being passionate all the time. Sometimes it's even more fun necking. We're considerate of each other's feelings. I had a tendency—men, I guess, have—to be selfish. But I stopped—I don't do that now. We try to be patient--and we are patient, gentle with each other. Maybe it's just not meant to be enjoyable with women you love.

JONATHAN

Sandy, you want to get laid?

SANDY

Please.

Cut to:

Exterior: tennis court—day

Angle on BOBBIE and CINDY sitting on a bench on the side of the court. CINDY, dark, sleek, watches avidly. BOBBIE reads the *Ladies' Home Journal*. Lying crumpled on the back of the bench next to CINDY is SANDY's sweater.

Sound: The tennis game.

SANDY

I almost had it!

CINDY groans and shakes her head. BOBBIE looks up.

SANDY

I almost had it, right, Cindy?!

CINDY smiles at SANDY. BOBBIE goes back to her reading.

Sound: The tennis game.

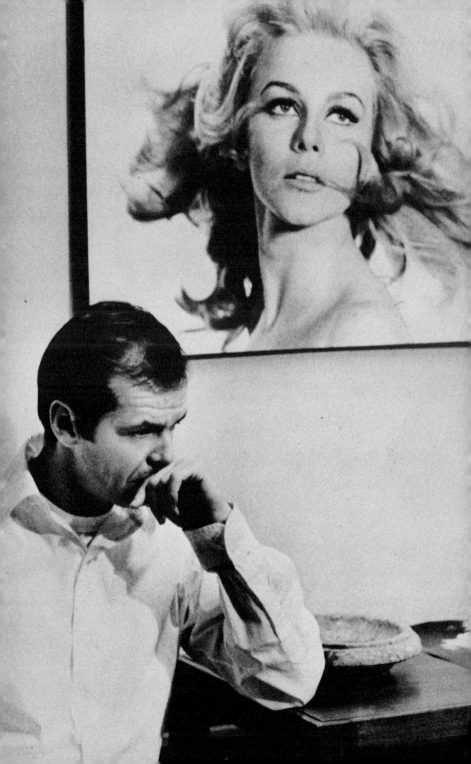

CINDY follows the game, jumps up in excitement.

> SANDY
>
> You see that, Cindy?!

> JONATHAN
>
> He was lucky!

CINDY grins. BOBBIE starts to look up, yawns, forgets and goes back to the *Ladies' Home Journal.*

Sound: The tennis game.

BOBBIE looks away.

> JONATHAN
>
> Bastard! That was out!

> SANDY
>
> Bullshit it was!

Follow BOBBIE as she rises and starts walking slowly away.

> JONATHAN
>
> Let Cindy be the judge!

> SANDY
>
> We'll do it over. All right?

> JONATHAN
>
> Fair's fair.

BOBBIE stands smoking, looking outside the fence.

Sound: The tennis game.

> JONATHAN
>
> Deuce! You see that shot, Cindy?

Sound: The tennis game.

SANDY

Dammit!

JONATHAN

Ad in! You see that, Cindy?

Sound: The tennis game.

BOBBIE sits and watches for a moment. She stifles a yawn.
CINDY doesn't seem to know she's there.

JONATHAN

Game!

SANDY

Luck!

JONATHAN

Luck, my ass! Want to take me on, Cindy?

CINDY jumps up. BOBBIE puts aside her magazine.

BOBBIE

It's my turn.

She rises.

JONATHAN

Oh, come on, Bobbie. You're so *awful*.

SANDY comes over to the bench, picks up his sweater, and
sits near BOBBIE.

Sound: The tennis game.

Shot: Close-up—Bobbie

She is staring at the game but her eyes gradually lose their
concentration.

JONATHAN

Very nice! You play well—hey, Sandy, will you look at this girl?

SANDY

Terrific, Cindy!

JONATHAN

Hey, she's racking me up, will you look at this?—I'm not kidding. She's racking me up.

SANDY

Beautiful!

JONATHAN

Hey, come on, is this something? Forty–love! And I'm not taking it easy on her either.

BOBBIE appears to be in a trance.

Cut to:

Interior: Jonathan's bathroom—evening

JONATHAN stands under the shower. Through the shower door he watches BOBBIE enter the bathroom, naked, and wash her face. The sink water cuts into his shower water and he glowers with suppressed rage. BOBBIE leaves the bathroom, reenters, and proceeds to make up her face.

JONATHAN enters the bedroom and begins rummaging through the dresser drawers. He picks a bill off the top of the dresser and reads it.

JONATHAN

You and Lord and Taylor's are going to have to work out a trial separation.

BOBBIE

(Opens the bathroom door) I had the water running, what did you say?

JONATHAN

You and Lord and Taylor's are going to have to work out a trial separation.

She reaches for the bill.

BOBBIE

Look at the date.

JONATHAN

What do you mean?

BOBBIE

Five months ago.

They continue to dress in silence.

BOBBIE

I'm sorry I cost you so much money.

She sips a drink. The phone rings. Neither answers. The phone stops. BOBBIE stops dressing and just sits. JONATHAN looks over at her, goes to her, fondles and kisses her.

BOBBIE

I want to get married.

He enters the bathroom and loudly slams the door. She sips her drink. After a moment, he exits from the bathroom, then quickly reenters, this time leaving the door open.

BOBBIE

Are you tired of me, Jonathan?

JONATHAN

(Under his breath) Am I ever.

BOBBIE

The answer is yes.

JONATHAN

I didn't say yes.

He returns to the bedroom.

BOBBIE

You said, "Am I ever." I need more in life than this.

JONATHAN

Who put you up to this? Your psychiatrist? After a long exhaustive bed-hunt, you've chosen me.

BOBBIE

Cindy's not a virgin either.

JONATHAN

What? Oh, I get it! Is that what brought this on? Your mind is unbelievable! You really have to have a low opinion of me—thinking I'd do that to Sandy.

BOBBIE

No, you wouldn't want to cheat on Sandy.

JONATHAN

Oh-ho—now it's Sandy.

BOBBIE

He spends half his life over here.

JONATHAN

Wait a minute—a second ago you had me screwing Cindy. Who'm I screwing now? Sandy?

BOBBIE

You're going too fast for me.

JONATHAN

I'm going too fast for *you!* That little mind of yours operates like an IBM—like a pinball machine. First Cindy—oh, not Cindy? How about Sandy? How about Cindy *and* Sandy? Talk about the pot calling the kettle. The day I got an earful of your checkered past I felt like a celibate.

BOBBIE

You made me tell you.

JONATHAN

Sure—I twisted your arm.

BOBBIE

It got you hot.

JONATHAN

Well, something has to!

He slams into the bathroom. She slumps onto the bed for a moment. She takes a pill out of a bottle on the bed-table and downs it with her drink. He stalks out of the bathroom.

BOBBIE

You have such contempt for me.

JONATHAN

Kid, you worked hard for it, it's yours.

BOBBIE

The way you paw me at parties.

JONATHAN

Now affection is contempt. Upside down. Everything upside down.

BOBBIE

Feeling me up in public is not affection.

JONATHAN

Will you come on!

BOBBIE

I know I sleep all day—I know I'm doing a terrible job—but you're not helping me any.

JONATHAN

And who helps me?

BOBBIE

I help you.

JONATHAN

Your kind of help I can do without.

BOBBIE

Oh, can you? Can you, really?

He charges into and out of the bathroom. He has on a new tie.

JONATHAN

You'll do anything you can to ruin my day, won't you? I got up feeling so good—*(He rips off his tie and starts changing shirts)* You couldn't leave us alone. We were doing so well—

BOBBIE

What?!

JONATHAN

At one time! At one time it was great what we had. The kidding around. It can't have a natural time span? Affairs can't dissolve in a good way? There's always got to be poison? I don't see why. I really don't see why.

BOBBIE

Jonathan, you want it to be over between us?

JONATHAN

Why does it have to be one way or the other?

BOBBIE

You don't want me to leave.

JONATHAN

I want you right here, where you belong.

BOBBIE

And what about you?

JONATHAN

When I'm here I'm here, when I'm not here I'm there.

BOBBIE

Where?

JONATHAN

Wherever.

BOBBIE

No. I'm a man-eater, a ball-buster and a castrater. I want to get married.

JONATHAN

Where the fuck is my shoehorn?! This place is a mess. There's never any food in the house, half the time you look like you fell out of bed—you're in bed more than any other human being past the age of six months that I ever heard of—

BOBBIE

The reason I sleep all day is I can't stand my life.

JONATHAN

What life?

BOBBIE

Sleeping all day.

She laughs.

JONATHAN

(Smiles) You do that sort of thing, I love you all over
again.

BOBBIE

Marry me, Jonathan. Please marry me.

JONATHAN

You're trying to kill me!

BOBBIE

Marriage isn't death.

JONATHAN

Why *now?!*

BOBBIE

Because two years ago I slept eight hours, a year ago
it was twelve, now it's up to fifteen, pretty soon it's
gonna be twenty-four!

JONATHAN

What are you trying to do—scare me?

She takes a pill and downs it with Scotch.

BOBBIE

I need a life.

JONATHAN

Get a job!

BOBBIE
I don't want a job, I want you!

JONATHAN
I'm taken. By *me!* Get out of the house, goddamn it
—do something useful.

BOBBIE
You wouldn't let me work when I wanted to.

JONATHAN
That was a year ago.

BOBBIE
You throw a tantrum every time you call and I'm
not home.

JONATHAN
Look, sister, I'm out there in the jungle eight hours
a day.

BOBBIE
You wouldn't even let me canvass for Kennedy!

JONATHAN
You want a job? I got a job for you—fix up this goddamn pigsty. Listen, you get a pretty goddamn good
salary for testing out that bed all day. You want another fifty a week? Try vacuuming. You want an
extra hundred? Try making the bed. Try opening
some windows! That's why you can hardly stand up.
The goddamn place smells like a coffin!

She takes a pill, downs it with Scotch.

JONATHAN
Bobbie, you don't need me. Why do you take this
kind of abuse? Walk out! Leave me! Please leave me,
Bobbie. I'd almost marry you if you'd leave me.

He goes to her. She takes him in her arms.

BOBBIE

You call that abuse? You don't know what I'm used to. With all your carrying on, to me, Jonathan, you're a gift. *(Pause)* So what's it gonna be?

He pulls abruptly away.

JONATHAN

You really know how to screw things up.

BOBBIE

So where does that leave us?

JONATHAN

You giving me an ultimatum?

She doesn't answer.

JONATHAN

Is this an ultimatum? Answer me, you ball-busting, castrating, son-of-a-cunt bitch! Is this an ultimatum or not? Well, I'll tell you what you can do with your ultimatum! I'll tell you what you can do with it!

He starts ripping the bed apart.

JONATHAN

You can make the goddamn bed! That's what you can do with it! You can change these filthy sheets—

The doorbell rings. He turns panic-stricken toward the sound of the bell.

Cut to:

Interior: Jonathan's hallway

JONATHAN swings open the door and stares, wild-eyed, at SANDY and CINDY dressed for a party.

> JONATHAN
> *She's not ready!*

SANDY looks at him.

> SANDY
> Well, we're a little early.

They move into the living room.

> JONATHAN
> You look good, Cindy.

She smiles coolly.

> SANDY
> I do my best.

JONATHAN and SANDY exchange smiles.

> CINDY
> Will Bobbie be long?

> JONATHAN
> Hey, do we have to go to this party?

> SANDY
> How about it, Cindy?

CINDY rises with her handbag.

> CINDY
> Where's the powder room?

JONATHAN points.

CINDY

I'm going. You do what you want.

She goes off.

JONATHAN

Man, she's really something.

SANDY

I'm so bored I'm going out of my mind.

JONATHAN

Bored? With that? You must be kidding. You have
to go to this party? Stick around.

SANDY

No, it's better that I go.

CINDY comes back. SANDY reaches out to pull her to him.
She evades him.

CINDY

Hey! I just did my hair.

She goes over to the phonograph and examines JONATHAN's
records.

CINDY

I got this at home. How's your tennis game, Jonathan?

JONATHAN

We'll have to have a rematch.

CINDY

Any time.

She puts on a cha-cha record, turns it up loud, picks up a
copy of *Vogue* and, swaying slightly in beat to the music,
begins leafing through it.

JONATHAN picks up his drink and SANDY follows him with his drink into the kitchen. He goes to the refrigerator and starts taking ice out of trays.

JONATHAN

(*Low*) Is she always that way?

SANDY

You know women.

JONATHAN

Boy, is she competitive.

SANDY

She is very competitive. But I find that attractive.

JONATHAN

You know what her problem is? She wants balls.

SANDY

She's all right.

JONATHAN

I'm not criticizing.

SANDY

I wish she were more feminine.

JONATHAN

She's a little masculine.

SANDY

I just wish she wouldn't always demand her own way.

JONATHAN

She's got a great body on her.

SANDY

I have to treat her like a child, give her everything she wants.

I wouldn't mind giving her something.

SANDY

You've got Bobbie. I should only have it that good.

JONATHAN

Oh, I don't know—

SANDY

Bobbie? Are you kidding? I've never seen a body like that.

JONATHAN

She could do with a little more of what Cindy's got. She's so goddamn passive.

SANDY

Yeah? I wouldn't mind Cindy just lying still once. She's so busy handing out instructions in bed it's like a close-order drill.

JONATHAN

Yeah? I wouldn't mind a little of that. As long as she doesn't forget who's boss. Hey, you wouldn't want to swap sometime, would you?

SANDY chuckles. JONATHAN chuckles.

SANDY

You serious?

JONATHAN

What do you say? It might liven things up a bit.

SANDY looks uncertain.

JONATHAN

She can miss one party. Leave her to me.

SANDY

What about Bobbie?

JONATHAN

She's so mad at me, she'll jump all over you just to get revenge.

SANDY laughs nervously.

JONATHAN

You like that, huh?

SANDY

Seriously—

JONATHAN

She's in the bedroom. If you're quiet, you can do it and she won't even know. *(He nudges him)*

SANDY

You bastard.

JONATHAN

Give me a minute.

Cut to:

Interior: Jonathan's living room

JONATHAN stares at CINDY, still swaying to the music and reading *Vogue*.

CINDY

Tell Sandy it's time to leave.

He goes to her and puts his hands on her hips. She drops the magazine and puts her arms on his shoulders.

CINDY

I hope you dance better than you play tennis.

They start to dance. He tries to kiss her. She pushes him
away. They dance a bit and he tries again. She pushes him
away again.

JONATHAN

Sandy won't mind.

CINDY

What's Sandy got to do with it?

JONATHAN

You're his girl.

She smiles.

JONATHAN

He said it would be okay.

She stops dancing.

CINDY

What did Sandy say?

She turns off the phonograph.

JONATHAN

That you and me—you know?

CINDY

That was his idea. You had nothing to do with it.

He smiles.

JONATHAN

A little.

CINDY

A little or a lot?

He spreads his hands.

JONATHAN

This much.

She gives him a long, measuring stare.

CINDY

I'm surprised it took you this long to get around to it. Tell Sandy we have a party to go to.

JONATHAN

(Grins) Sandy's busy.

She picks up her coat.

CINDY

You want to come around sometime by yourself, that's one thing. I've been expecting that. But you tell Sandy if he lays one hand on that tub of lard in there not to come home.

She opens the front door and turns to JONATHAN.

CINDY

So you call me.

She leaves. JONATHAN returns to the living room, lights a cigarette, starts to sit down. Suddenly:

JONATHAN

Jesus!

Follow him as he rushes to the bedroom.

What he sees

BOBBIE lies sprawled across the bed, unconscious. SANDY, still fully dressed, is speaking into the phone.

SANDY

She's semi-comatose. Better send a resuscitator and an airway. Who's on? Portis? Tell him to be ready to give her an I.V. on admission.

He stares coldly at JONATHAN. He picks up the empty pill container and holds it up for him to see.

SANDY

Bastard.

Follow JONATHAN as he turns and bolts out of the room, down the hall, and back into the living room. He stands for a moment, frozen.

JONATHAN

Very slick—very clever—*(He screams)*
It's not gonna work, Bobbie!

Cut to:

Slide screen

First slide: *Jonathan Fuerst Presents*

Second slide: *A Jonathan Fuerst Production*

Third slide: *Ball-busters On Parade!*

The slides change in sync with JONATHAN's commentary, beginning with crude black-and-white Brownie photos of children and concluding with stylish full-color pin-ups.

JONATHAN

That's Bonnie, my first love, she lived upstairs from us. We started exposing ourselves to each other at ten. We got caught on the roof one day by my mother. She washed my mouth out with soap. I never got the connection. Here's Emily—she was my first steady, until she moved off the block at eleven —I never laid a hand on her. Mildred, I think this one's name is—she followed me around in school. The fellows kidded me about her. I warned her I'd beat her up if she didn't stop. She picked up her skirt, dropped her pants, and shoved her ass at me— so my first sight of ass was at twelve. Here's Marcia, thirteen and a half or thereabouts—I kissed her at a Spin-the-Bottle party—

Pan off the screen to:

Interior: Jonathan's living room—dark

This is a new apartment, furnished mod, very cold. JONATHAN, working the slide projector, is dressed Madison Avenue semi-mod. His hair is thinning; he wears long sideburns; he looks bloated, in his forties. SANDY still looks boyish. He has let his hair grow very long, wears a buckskin jacket, bell bottoms, boots, and love beads. JENNIFER, sitting next to him, looks not much more than sixteen, is quite beautiful, with long hair reaching to her waist. Her dress is floor-length. Her feet are bare.

JONATHAN

This one's Rosalie. Rosalie looked like Elizabeth Taylor in *National Velvet*. I had a crush on Rosalie from fourteen to fifteen. I never went near her. In those days we had illusions.

Slide screen

JONATHAN

This is Charlotte. Not much on looks but great tits
for fifteen. That's Lenny Hartman's sister. My first
French kiss. Sixteen years old. Here's Gloria, the
best-built girl in Evander-Childs—I took her to the
Bronx Zoo once and on the bus copped a cheap feel.
Here's Gwen. I went with her almost a year trying
to get her to put out. But she thought I was too nice
and was saving me for marriage. Every guy in Evan-
der must have gotten into her pants except me.
Here we have my very first—

Slide screen: A split-second shot of SUSAN, on and off.

JONATHAN

No. That one's a mistake. Here's Eileen, my very
first fuck.

Slide screen

JONATHAN

She was a modern dancer at Swarthmore. Great
body on her but wasted, she was frigid. Here's Nancy.
A sweet kid—went into biology—very frigid.

BOBBIE flashes on the screen.

JONATHAN

Heeerrres Bobbie! My wife! The fastest tits in the
West, but king of the ball-busters. She conned me

into marrying her, now she's killing me with alimony. I don't know how this got mixed up in here, this is my little girl, Wendy—Princess I call her—isn't she a dreamboat? Here's a real cunt—I forget her name—a Nazi—I banged her in Berlin. Here's something I went with for a couple of months—I forget her name—first time I banged her was in a yacht race to Nassau. This slob I lived with a year until I got so sick of her ball-busting I couldn't get it up. This was my Jap-in-the-sack. I heard that Oriental girls were different. Not in America, they're not. Here's a sixteen-year-old I paid twenty bucks to one night when I was drunk in the Village—maybe you know her, Jennifer—she gave me a dose.

The screen goes blank.

> JONATHAN
> Th—th—th—that's all folks.

Angle on Sandy and Jennifer

JONATHAN switches the lights on. SANDY is numb with horror. JENNIFER is in tears. They get up slowly.

> JONATHAN
> What are you crying for? It's not a Lassie movie.

Angle on Jonathan and Sandy

An awkward exchange of stares.

SANDY and JENNIFER back their way toward the door.

110

Cut to:

Exterior: the city at night

JONATHAN and SANDY walking. It is cold, very dark. They walk in silence.

Sound: Traffic.

> JONATHAN
>
> Sorry about that. *(Pause)* Or something.

> SANDY
>
> So what else is new?

> JONATHAN
>
> I'll tell you the truth, I don't see anybody any more.

> SANDY
>
> Neither do we.

> JONATHAN
>
> *(Ironic)* Well, you have each other. I thought she was your daughter when you first came in.

> SANDY
>
> In a lot of ways she's older than I am.

> JONATHAN
>
> Yeah.

> SANDY
>
> She knows worlds I can't even begin to touch yet.

> JONATHAN
>
> Sandy, please.

He smiles.

SANDY

I found out who I am.

JONATHAN

You're in big trouble.

SANDY

Same old Jonathan.

JONATHAN

Indubitably.

SANDY

Let me talk to her about you, Jonathan.

JONATHAN

Talk to her about me? I'm forty, she's nine.

SANDY

You don't get it, do you?

JONATHAN

Oh, I get it, all right! I've been getting it for years! What's the point? *(Patiently)* Sandy, you found a good piece of ass. God bless you. You're my friend. I'm happy for you. As long as it lasts, I'm happy for you. You deserve happiness. I mean it. Why fight? Okay?

SANDY

All those games.

JONATHAN

Jesus Christ.

SANDY

You don't need those games, Jonathan. I know! I played more games than anybody! The obedient-son game, the bright-student game, the cocksman game—

Some cocksman.

SANDY

—The respectable-husband game, the good-father game—

JONATHAN lets out a bitter laugh.

JONATHAN

Good father?!

SANDY

—The specialist game. Games don't impress Jennifer. Just life. Just love.

JONATHAN

Yeah? Well, I don't want to argue, Sandy. So let's agree not to agree. Don't make me mad. Okay?

SANDY

Jennifer knows more at twenty than Susan knows to this day.

JONATHAN

You found yourself a jewel. Okay?

SANDY

She's my love teacher.

JONATHAN

Finally got it up, huh?

SANDY

You give off such bad vibrations.

JONATHAN

"Bad vibrations." Sandy, I love you, but you're a schmuck. Well, you were always young, Sandy. Open. You were schmucky a lot of the time but maybe schmuckiness is what you need to stay young and open. Listen, don't listen to me. You're doing great and I'm making money.

SANDY

You can find what I found, Jonathan.

JONATHAN

Don't make me insult you.

Cut to:

Interior: Louise's apartment—night

LOUISE's door swings open. LOUISE, about thirty-five, stands in a bathrobe, nothing on underneath. JONATHAN brushes past her into the apartment.

JONATHAN

Women!

LOUISE

All ball-busters, right?

JONATHAN

You know it. When you think of what he's got to dip into, any guy with a conscience has a right to turn soft. Am I right, Louise?

LOUISE

You're always right, lover.

She hands him a drink, then kisses him.

LOUISE

I don't think we're going to have any trouble tonight.

JONATHAN

You don't?

LOUISE

No, I don't.

JONATHAN

Are you sure?

LOUISE

Wanna bet?

JONATHAN

How much?

LOUISE

Sky's the limit.

JONATHAN

Goddammit!

He pulls away from her.

LOUISE

What did I do?

JONATHAN

You're doing it all wrong!

LOUISE

I'm doing it like always.

JONATHAN

You never said that before.

LOUISE

Said what?

JONATHAN

"Sky's the limit!"

Sure I did.

Never!

What do I say?

You forgot didn't you?

(*Remembering*) —"A hundred."

He begins to calm down.

I say "a hundred."

Okay.

It just came out.

I want it right, that's all.

A pause.

I don't think we're going to have any trouble to-night.

You don't?

No, I don't.

JONATHAN

Are you sure?

LOUISE

Wanna bet?

JONATHAN

How much?

LOUISE

A hundred?

JONATHAN

You sound pretty sure.

He takes a couple of bills from his trouser pocket and hands them to her. She puts them away.

LOUISE

Your kind of man? Why shouldn't I be sure?

JONATHAN

What kind of man am I?

LOUISE

A real man. A kind man.

JONATHAN

I'm not kind.

Close-up: Louise

During the course of the speech, she slowly sinks to her knees. We see her sinking, sinking, sinking, seemingly never to stop.

I don't mean weak-kind, the way so many men are. I mean the kindness that comes from enormous strength, from an inner power so strong that every act, no matter what, is more proof of that power. That's what all women resent. That's why they try to cut you down. Because your knowledge of yourself—and them—is so right, so true that it exposes the lies which they, every scheming one of them, live by. It takes a true woman to understand that the purest form of love is to love a man who denies himself to her. A man who inspires worship because he has no need for any woman—*because he has himself!* And who is better? More beautiful, more powerful, more perfect—you're getting hard—more strong, more masculine, more extraordinary, more robust—it's rising, it's rising!—more virile, more domineering, more irresistible—it's up! *It's in the air!*